No Love Lost

How I Survived Grief and Found Hope Again Through Love, Faith, and Support

Summyr Wright-Nelson

Dedication

This book is dedicated to my personal angel, my first born, my first gift that ushered me into motherhood in a unique way, vastly different than most, but motherhood that an entire community of women understand.

Thank you for existing, son. Thank you for helping Mommy dig a little deeper and heal wounds that she didn't even know were there. You led me to become the mother I am to your beautiful little sister. I believe I truly am blossoming as a woman because of you. God is still faithful and I hope both you and God are pleased with this body of work.

I will never let you be forgotten. Anytime someone asks me if your sister is my first I always confidently say no, we have a son in heaven, just so the world knows you were here. I love you so much.

Now, Mommy will probably still cry over you from time to time but I know that any tear I shed is just a representation of the deep love I have for you.

CONTENTS

PREFACE

I wake up around 7:00 am feeling as though I've been hit by a train. I lay back down and later get up for real around 9:30 am. My stomach is now oddly settled; my baby isn't moving. He usually moves as soon as I wake up. Now eight months pregnant, I know at least that much for sure. I'm not one for counting kicks because he moves often, and he was moving nonstop all night. I don't want to be meticulous or overreact, as I've already been obsessing over everything else concerning our baby's arrival: his clothes, his mattress, his bottles, the latest baby devices, etc., constantly researching and doing everything in my power to prepare the best life possible for my baby. I spent each day of my pregnancy poring over every little detail of what life would be like with our new little addition.

If enjoying every bit of your pregnancy was a person, it was me. So when I woke up that morning, I immediately knew something was wrong. But I didn't know what it was.

And I definitely never thought my day would end the way it did.

Chapter 1:
The Journey to Motherhood

Prior to getting pregnant, I'd been having some health challenges from around late 2018 to late 2020. I went to numerous doctors and specialists who gave different "diagnoses" including a lazy colon, adrenal fatigue, and hormone imbalances. I even had cysts on my ovaries at one point. I had numerous symptoms such as major hair loss and thinning. My scalp was very sensitive and felt like it was on fire all the time. My hair texture changed. I was so tired sometimes that no matter how much rest I got I would catch myself falling asleep at traffic lights and be awakened by car horns. I had constant brain fog, skin breakouts, random rashes, frequent pelvic and back pain. The pain was so excruciating at times I couldn't wear jeans because I couldn't take the pressure against my pelvis. I couldn't stand for long periods of time without feeling like I had a million needles piercing my legs to the point of numbness. I constantly felt weak. My confidence started to dwindle and my mental health was affected. I began to realize that I was dealing with depression and anxiety simultaneously.

With each disappointing doctor's visit, my finances dwindling from paying out of pocket for answers, and collecting more debt, I contemplated dying. I didn't want to harm myself, but I was tired of fighting for my health. I wanted to give up. In fact I did. I even gave up on acting. I started turning down gigs and making up excuses. I made a decision to let the pain continue to overwhelm my body and I would just hold on until it either worked itself out or it didn't. One day I had a dream during a midday nap on a Saturday afternoon. God showed me a vision of me driving a car at night in my hometown up a hill with my husband (then fiancé) in the passenger seat. When I got to the top of the hill, the car shut off and we started rolling back. In the dream I knew we would crash if I didn't figure out how to gain control of the car again. Then I woke up and prayed. It was revealed to me that my health challenges were temporary. I still had a life to live and was literally still accelerating upward in other areas. If I gave up, I'd just let my entire life go downhill and deep down, I honestly didn't want that at all.

Also, I wasn't alone. I had support. I was so used to trying to figure things out on my own out of survival that I didn't even consider I had a whole man I was engaged to that could support me through this if I allowed him to. Shortly after I made up my mind to not give up, I started going to therapy. I started praying more and fighting for healing in my body while still going after my dreams which resulted in booking a three day all expense paid print gig in Charleston, SC that I didn't even apply for and I was flown to Atlanta for a Producer session with Tyler Perry Studios still not feeling 100% but totally trusting God was going to heal me. Thank God I didn't give up and I took heed to what God was trying to tell me. Those experiences gave me hope and let me know I was moving in the right direction. I started channeling my pain into my art as an actor with every audition or new opportunity and that was healing. I started to believe, see, and speak my healing into existence, even when I faced more disappointments. I had hope. My mindset was changing. Little by little, I started doing holistic things like adding more nutrients in my daily diet, meditating, speaking life over myself, seeing a chiropractor, getting acupuncture, cupping, trying Chinese medicine methods, etc. I started gaining my strength back, I was able to work out again, and I could wear what I wanted. There was no more pain in my legs, I could stand and walk without numbness, and the cysts cleared on my ovaries. I still had gastrointestinal issues, brain fog, and my scalp would hurt every now and then. But I was progressing, which was good.

One day in August 2020 it dawned on me that everything I was dealing with prior to and at the present time most likely stemmed from my gut. I say it dawned on me but I know now this was the Holy Spirit. Constipation was the one consistent issue I've had my entire life. I just learned to live with it, thinking I had IBS. But I was determined to get to the bottom of what was going on with me, so I found one more GI specialist at Johns Hopkins. She ran every test imaginable– tests no doctor, let alone a GI specialist, ever thought to run on me or had access to.

We ultimately discovered I had Lazy Bowel Syndrome, which meant that once food reached my large intestine it slowed down tremendously and didn't break down foods at a normal transit time. Yet, I was told I was born this way and that there wasn't much that could be done beyond pelvic floor therapy to help strengthen my bowel muscles and retrain my body on the proper way to poop. I thought to myself: how am I dealing with geriatric bowels in my 20's? Make it make sense! But it could've been worse, so I was thankful I could at least manage it. When I told my husband about it he said, "So you mean to tell me you've been dealing with all that stuff for this long because you're full of shit?" It's ok, you can laugh – I did. He then said "My bad, I couldn't help it. That was a good one, huh?" It was.

But truth be told, this explained the years of constipation, amongst other things. Toxic waste must've been sitting in my system for such a long time that it started affecting other bodily functions and organs. If toxic waste isn't cleared out routinely, then let's just say Houston, you have a problem, which I learned through countless research. I could see in some of the scans they ran on me that the waste had been pressing on my pelvis and surrounding organs, which explained the pain.

From some of the changes I'd made previously I must've started moving some of it out of the way, but it wasn't enough. I knew pelvic floor therapy would be expensive because my insurance didn't cover it at the time, but I was willing to make it work. One day before starting therapy I found a woman that did colon hydrotherapy in Baltimore. This was something I was familiar with having done several times throughout the years for relief. This woman seemed different more knowledgeable and advanced technology. I booked with her and she was a believer she was able to feel that I needed more than just that one session. We connected and as a new herbalist as well she offered to make me a batch of herbal teas to aid in my healing and help flush some extra waste out. I did this for a few weeks. I believe it was helpful. Then one day on Instagram I came across a page entitled @iamsurvivingvegan. I saw that she'd created a full body detox to help people rid themselves of toxic waste and parasites. I purchased it and my entire life changed. Let me tell you the truth that detox was hard with a capital H. I wanted to give up on day 5 but I didn't I knew the end result I wanted to get to. After completing the 10-day raw vegan detox she'd crafted, I was able to go to the bathroom regularly: something I hadn't been able to do for years. I felt lighter, my brain fog was gone, and it must've even cleared up some things in the reproductive area because I also had a newfound sex drive. My lady parts could've been nicknamed Niagara Falls, which explains us conceiving on day 7 of the detox! That cleanse changed my life. I felt completely healed internally from utilizing the very things God placed on this earth. It was as if someone hit the reset button in my body and turned on the master light switch.

I believe I went through all that for a reason. It was a faith journey, and God healed me by leading me to the answers I needed because I chose to believe I could be healed and refused to give up. Little did I know I would embark on yet another journey of faith with this new life growing inside of me.

Chapter 2: The Joys of Pregnancy

Before I knew it myself, I found out I was pregnant through a prophet.

I won't mention her name but I'm very grateful for her and the timing in which she was introduced to my life. She's probably between the age of my mother, who's 50 years young, and my grandmother, who is 67. (My mother may not appreciate me sharing that but it's done now, Mom. Love you!). This woman was from the South like me and was so honest and easy to talk to. She felt like family. Not only did she confirm some things I had been contemplating, but she knew a lot about me before even laying eyes on me. So I knew she was hearing from God. She said, "There's a child. Who has a child? Are you pregnant?" I quickly replied, "Me? Oh no, definitely not." She replied, "Ok, but I just keep seeing a child and it's very close." Again, I replied, "Yeah, no. It's not me. Maybe someone I know, but I'm definitely not pregnant." She just said ok and we moved on. I'm thinking, *"Lady . . . I would know. I'm not sick. I have no signs or symptoms of pregnancy."*

But a week later, I missed my period. I woke up before even taking a pregnancy test and wrote in my journal, thanking God for this new life growing inside of me. I had this unexplainable peace that came over me. I just started thanking God for this blessing in advance and then continued my day as usual. An hour before my husband was supposed to get off from work, I jetted out to my silver Nissan Sentra and went to the nearest grocery store up the street, which happened to be a Harris Teeter.

I didn't know where the tests were located in the store. I went to the pharmacy to ask a woman standing at the counter and she gave me a slightly judgmental stare, topped with an *"Aww, poor thing"* type of look as she muttered out that I could find them on Aisle 8. I politely told her thanks, but in my head I was thinking "*I probably look like a teenager to her but dang, she didn't have to give me all that energy! Even if I was super young, so what?"* But then I let it go because I realized looking super young is a good thing! "*Come on, good genes!"* I thought to myself. *"She wishes she could look this young!"* (See how I just turned a negative to a positive in my head like that? I know there was a little shade in it, but I digress).

By the time I wrapped up that thought in my head, I'd reached the aisle with all the feminine products and the slew of pregnancy test brands. I started Googling which one to buy. FIRST RESPONSE™ was number one on the list but Clearblue® Digital was a close second, so I just went with that one. I didn't have time to see a faint second line and still be unsure. I needed a test to give it to me straight. Plus, I had already missed my period so I felt it would be accurate. I got home and decided to take it right before my husband returned from work.

Side Note: make sure you carefully read the directions because it's really important that you pee on the stick midstream for five seconds so you get an accurate read.

I put the stick on top of the counter and left it. I'm pretty sure I watched a show for like five minutes to distract me. When I went back to the bathroom to check, sure enough the test read: **Pregnant.** Now at this point it was all confirmed for me. I didn't question if I had a faulty test or anything. I knew in my spirit and it also helped that I had received a prophetic confirmation a week prior.

When my husband came home, I was in the bathroom feeling so amped that I had to tell him right then. The most creative thing I could think to do was put the test in my pocket and trick him into doing a TikTok dance with me and on one of the moves I'd reach in my pocket and show it to him. So that's what I did. I came out of the bathroom and he was lying on the couch. I set up my phone to record but told him we have to practice first so I had him turn on the song to the dance we were going to do so I could teach him the moves. (This was the only way me recording wouldn't look suspicious). By dance move #2, I whipped out the test and handed it to him. As I reflect now, this sounds like a total ambush and not that well planned but hey, it was spontaneous and I'm good for that!

So he took it and said "What is this?" I told him, "It's a pregnancy test. I'm pregnant." He gave it back to me and said, "Why are you playing? No, you're not. This is a joke." I thought to myself, *"Dang, this was not the reaction I was going for. Didn't see this coming."* He starts laughing and says, "You're definitely playing right now and I'm not doing this one with you." I reiterated to him that I was serious. He finally asked if I could pee on another stick. I'm like, wow, this really took a turn. But looking back, I get it. Devon and I make TikToks all the time and some of them have been jokes so I can see how he would think I was on joke time. The thing is this is the one thing I'd never joke about because I knew how much he wanted to be a father. He had expressed to me that this was his lifelong dream. We've been talking about kids since we were in college but that was NOT going down back then. But that conversation is for an entirely different book . . .

Eventually, I threw my hands up and stopped trying to convince him because we were running short on time before a photoshoot I had booked that day for a clothing line. Thank God it was still early on, so everything still fit as normal. I got dressed in a yellow tailored suit with my curls styled in a fresh wash-and-go and my make-up done. We got in the car and took a 40-minute ride up the road to get to this photoshoot. At the shoot he kept looking at me and smiling. I knew he believed me then. I think he may have been in shock the entire time. Maybe me telling him the way I did without having mentioned the possibility made it all feel surreal for him initially. For me, it was the complete opposite. Reality hit me immediately after reading *Pregnant* on that blue and white stick.

On the ride home we didn't really talk about it because we were also in the middle of looking for a house, so most of that ride was spent on the phone with our lender and realtor discussing "house stuff." When we got back home to our apartment the baby conversation resumed. He was in a good mood. I took the last test just to ease any inkling that I could've still been joking. His excitement turned up a notch and we shared a lingering sweet intimate hug. You know the kind where you can't stop rubbing the other person's back, followed by three sweet kisses on the lips. Well, that's our thing–it must be three every time. So here we were becoming parents! I reassured him that I'd joked about a lot of things before but never about this. I knew how much becoming a father meant to him. This moment we shared matured us some, and deepened our empathy and intimacy for one another as husband and wife.

Now many of you may be reading this and wondering if we were trying to become pregnant. The answer is no, but we weren't trying to prevent it either. After our public wedding on March 7, 2020 for lack of better terms we agreed that he could shoot the club up! Which means he didn't have to pull out or use a condom. It was a big deal for us when we made that decision. We had already officially gotten married at the courthouse in January, and started having protected sex after being celibate for 2.5 years prior. (I was not trying to pop up pregnant at my actual wedding, it's just not what I personally wanted). But even after our wedding, it wasn't until months later while on the full body detox that we popped up pregnant so it didn't happen overnight. It was a process. And I could see the hand of God every step of the way.

♦♦♦

From the time I discovered I was pregnant, it was on! I was totally obsessed with everything baby-related. I was watching YouTube videos every single day on what a baby needs, stages of pregnancy,and the best things I could get for our child. One thing I was very conscious about throughout my pregnancy was eating extremely healthy. Now, I take that back. I didn't eat *extremely* healthy food, but I ate healthy for the most part. I definitely binged on vegan pizza quite a bit and even though it was vegan, that was still a lot of bread, and probably a good bit of sodium. And I did eat meat during that pregnancy despite being vegan up until I got pregnant. I was craving a lot of meat: ground chicken and lots of turkey bacon. I didn't eat pork, beef, or anything like that but definitely chicken and fish. My appetite was very good and I feel like I ate healthy for the most part. I took my prenatal vitamins regularly and drank my water, so that wasn't an issue.

I also exercised a lot. (Ok, I lied). But during the second trimester, I started to exercise a bit more. I had an app on my phone that was specifically for exercising while pregnant. I walked a lot during my second and third trimester. My first trimester, I didn't do much. As soon as I found out I was pregnant, I wanted to keep being active so I went running. And I remember I came home and I was about to faint. I literally had to crawl on the floor and just lay there awhile and cool off so I realized I can't push myself the way that I did before I was pregnant. My body just wasn't having it and at that point I was only like four or five weeks pregnant. My body was already telling me, "Girl, sit down."

But I got a burst of energy in my second trimester and I thought, "Oooh girl if you want to prepare yourself and be in good shape for when you're not pregnant anymore, you probably should work out." So I did. And I think that had a lot to do with the way that I healed postpartum.

♦♦♦

I didn't wait very long before announcing. I remember around Christmas-time I was only 12 weeks along and my mother was here (she's always here!). She flew into town to spend Christmas with us in our first apartment. She took our baby reveal picture upstairs in our loft and we were so excited to announce it that day, we sent that picture to all of our family and then put it on Instagram. It had such a great response and everyone seemed so invested with our journey at that point.

I started taking content creation more seriously because I wasn't working and I'm not one to just sit around and do nothing. I had to figure out ways to work on things I wanted to do. If I couldn't act because I was now pregnant, then I needed to figure out another creative outlet. I started creating TikToks and documenting my journey on Instagram by doing fun reels with my husband or just talking about my pregnancy. It was fun!

All throughout my first trimester we started making major preparations. We bought a three bedroom condo and remodeled it exactly how we wanted to so we could welcome our new child. I started an Etsy shop and I made motherhood-inspired mugs and T-shirts. I was even considering creating unique items for babies because I was so excited to be on this journey of motherhood.

I then hired a doula to add to the team to help educate and guide us. Because everything was normal, my doula and I agreed that it would be fine to switch to a birthing center with an experienced midwifery team. Everything was going great. I toured my birthing room and the porcelain white tub I'd be birthing in. I planned on having a dreamy atmosphere to deliver in. I envisioned my experience in that room with lavender painted walls, dim lighting , and a sweet aroma from essential oils in the air. My husband was going to have his arms draped around my shoulders , holding me as comfort, and whispering encouraging words that only he would know how to form in order to bring me to complete calmness. I would be completely free of medical intervention, allowing my body to feel every surge while I ride each wave alongside my husband, doula , and midwifery team. They would be encouraging my strength to shine through every surge and then through every push, then out would come my beautiful baby boy. I would be proud of the way I conquered birthing my first human. I was going to be reborn into a new woman. I was going to birth exactly the way I always imagined I would. Yet, my reality couldn't have been any more the opposite of what I dreamed for myself, my baby, and my husband. I thought we would have the luxury of utilizing the bed provided as I recovered and walk into the lobby with our newborn as we prepared to check out and go home as other expectant mothers approached the desk for their next appointment as this was once me watching a mother hold her newborn on the gray couch in the lobby.

One day, I called the prophetess back to let her know that I was indeed pregnant. I also found out the baby's gender through her. She literally started praying for my son. I found that out because she kept saying, "he." *He's gonna be this and he's gonna be that. He's gonna be a prophet and he's gonna mend families.* So when you hear something like that, automatically there's no way I'm thinking, "I'm gonna lose my son." If my son is supposed to have this huge impact and do all of these things and be a prophet and do all of that, he's gotta make it here, right? I had no fear because I had this prophet who ensured me the greatness that comes with my son, down to her revealing things about other people and praying off negative things. It was just very interesting. She let me know this was a time to sit still and let God do his thing and let my husband totally lead and support. Before finding out I was pregnant I had just locked in new management for my acting career. A manager I wanted for a while and we were on a roll with great auditions coming through. My husband always wanted to give me the opportunity to only focus on acting while he took care of all of our bills. That made me nervous at first because I love contributing but who wouldn't relish in that type of relief to only do what your hearts desires if your partner was more than willing to hold it down. He really believes in me! That taught me a big lesson – surrounding my husband - it was my season to allow him to flourish in that leadership role for our family and he does that very well. That's a good man Savannah! Ok, let me not start cutting up too much. Honestly, it was a huge turn on and he never once made me feel less than. He always used words like "ours" "we" "us." Surrendering to that season God had me in humbled me, built my trust in my husband's leadership, and strengthened our marriage because we had to be transparent about everything since we merged our finances.

Things were moving right along when it came time for our baby shower. We planned on having two: one in Augusta, GA, where I'm from, and one here in D.C where we lived, that one of my really good friends was going to host at a later date. My mother and best friend Alexis planned the baby shower in Augusta, and it was an absolute dream. Devon and I had driven down from D.C. to Augusta, an 8-hour trip in the car. I had just gotten my long knotless braids done right before we left. I was ready and prepared for this baby to come any day now.

At the time of the baby shower, I was 31 weeks pregnant, still very mobile, and still doing making TikTok videos. It was a celebration like no other and every part of it, down to the little details, was stunning. Never once did I feel ill or like something was wrong. I did feel like I had a knot in my butt from riding in the car for a very long time but other than that, Baby was moving a lot. It was a beautiful time with family and friends who loved and supported us in this journey of parenthood.

I flew back home after the baby shower because I didn't want to stay in the car that long going back and everything was still good with baby boy. Shortly after that, my husband decided he wanted to go visit one of his friends for a book signing in Texas. So we prepared for his trip and flew my mom to D.C to stay with me. Since the trip was such short notice and I was so far along in my pregnancy, I didn't really want to be home alone knowing that children come when they want to come.

Mind you, I was pregnant at the same time as two other people I was really close to – my godsister, who was having a son, and one of my acting buddies, who was having a daughter – and also a few other women I knew from Instagram. (People on Instagram become like friends and even though you've never met, it's still so cool how you feel like you know them). My acting friend actually said she had a dream about me being pregnant, and we were only three weeks apart. So here I was with two women I could relate to and we were having conversations back and forth like, "How was your appointment? Oh really? What did your doctor say?" My acting friend called me when she delivered her daughter early at 36 weeks. I was so excited like, "Oh my gosh, my turn is right around the corner." At that point I was 33 weeks. This made me really excited for my water birth. So here I was not thinking anything tragic was going to happen. I mean my friend JUST told me she delivered her baby. Surely I'd be calling her with the same news.

Thank God my mom was there with me because a couple of days later, I didn't have the same news my friend had.

Chapter 3: *The Day Everything Changed*

There's a scripture in the Bible that says, "Weeping may endure for a night, but joy comes in the morning." But for me, it felt like the night would never end. At least for a while.

I wake up one morning, 8 months pregnant, and I immediately know something is wrong, but I don't know what. I slowly get dressed, feeling very eerie. But I don't panic. I had already been to the hospital once, at 25 weeks, after a long weekend of birthday fun and not enough hydration. The doctor hooked me up to fluids and our baby got to bustin' all kinds of moves in my belly. I never skimped on my water supply after that day. So as you can imagine this particular morning (Sunday, May 23rd to be exact), I began doing all the things I know to do to get him moving. I drank over a gallon of water and eat foods that typically amp our baby up, to no avail. I go to my favorite nearby juice shop with my Mom, thinking a ginger shot should definitely work. It doesn't. I know my energy is off so I tell my Mom, "I'm sorry I'm no fun right now, I will be once I feel him move." She says, "Do you want to go to the hospital?" I reply, "No, I'm sure it's fine," and we continue the day I planned for us.

We are headed to eat, and while riding down the highway my Mother starts to feel really ill from a wheatgrass shot. I think to myself, *"That's odd . . . from wheatgrass?"* So I ask her if she wants to turn around and head back to my house. She says, "Yes, I just need to lay down for a little bit." We get home around 6:00 pm and before she goes to lay down she says, "Why don't you call your midwife and see if she has any advice?" So I do, and put her on speakerphone so my mom can hear, too. She tells me to drink 16 ounces of juice. I grab pineapple juice from the fridge and drink it. She tells me to wait a few minutes because as babies get bigger in the womb they may not move as much, so I may have to nudge him.

Ten minutes or more go by with no response from baby boy. She then instructs me to go lay down and push on my belly to wake him up. Again, nothing. Now

I'm starting to panic a tad, but not a lot because I don't want to send myself into a downward spiral unnecessarily. I still need to ensure my son is in a safe, stress-free environment inside of my womb. I believe he can feel everything I feel, so I want to protect him. I always wanted to protect him.

My midwife tells me to call the EMT to come get me because they will get me to the hospital without having to wait. The hospital process is always faster if an EMT takes you there. It works. They come, and she tells me she will meet us there. My mother jumps up and follows behind us to the hospital. We are still not thinking the worst right now. On the way, the EMT tells me about a pregnancy scare his wife had. She ended up having an autoimmune disease which passed something on to their daughter. It became difficult for the mother, but she still had a successful birth. No one figured anything like this would happen to me. He helps me remain calm. We laugh. We arrive. It's still daylight out.

I swiftly go through the hospital process. They take me into triage. This floor is pretty much empty. I'm alone. My husband is out of town and will be returning late that night. My mother is still parking the car. The first nurse hooks me up to the heartbeat monitor. She can't find anything. I'm still calm. Again I went through this with the whole dehydration scare and it took a minute but my boy got to going, so no worries here. The second nurse comes in and does the same thing. Again, nothing. Now they are headed out to get the doctor. Still no panic but I know something may be up. I mean, my life has never been a walk in the park anyway. Even in the midst of great joy or success, it seems like there's always something to overcome. Something always seems to happen right before a breakthrough for me, or right before I get over a hurdle.

The doctor comes into the room, sits on the edge of my hospital bed in front of a computer screen surrounded by the two nurses that were in my room previously. The doctor slowly turns around, places her hand gently on my leg, and stares at me with an immensely somber look in her eyes. I look through her soul and know within myself that whatever she's about to say is going to rock my world and not in a good way.

She begins to utter, “I have some really unfort- . . .” but I don’t hear the rest. All the sound around me fell to complete silence. I start to scream at the top of my lungs. Quivering out the words, “No, this is not happening to me. This is not happening to me. This can’t be real. This can’t be real.” My mother must have heard me screaming in the hall and that led her to me. All of a sudden as I’m completely blinded by the rush of tears in my eyes I feel this jolt of force from the embrace my mother greeted me with in the midst of my biggest tragedy. She held on to me so tightly as if she was trying to soak up my pain, but she couldn’t. No one could. She was in shambles. I was too, but then I dried up all my tears. I stared off at the wall straight in front of me. I think I may have gone numb. As a mother I decided I’m going to fight for my son’s life with everything I got left and from what I could do. I prayed for a miracle in my head. Now that I’ve calmed down, I listen to what the doctor had to say. She went on to tell me they couldn’t find my baby’s heartbeat. They tried and tried but it’s not there which means he has passed. Even though I just felt him that morning they said it could have happened in the 2.5 hour nap I took that morning. Of course that weighed on me. I questioned "Why didn't I just come earlier?" But in reality, there is nothing I could have done to stop it. I'm pretty sure this was the first time the nurses tending to had experienced a patient in this circumstance, they were in shambles. It was actually overwhelming emotionally to carry there emotions as well as min in that moment. My midwife eventually arrived to help counsel me through initial decisions with the doctor for my next steps.

As I walked down the long, bleak halls of the hospital where I just found out my baby no longer had a heartbeat, I had an odd sense of poise. Though disappointed by what I'd just experienced, I had somehow gathered myself. My mother had gone to pull my car up to the front of the hospital to take me back home. My midwife and I strolled along those halls into the elevator and she brought up one of the overdramatic nurses and we shared a laugh. I needed that little humor break. Having experienced child loss in a different way, she explained to me some things I may need to get through the night, and went to pick them up for me. As I got in the car with my mother, my odd poise shifted to nothingness. I felt like I was moving in the space of a reality that didn't belong to me, except it did.

My mother tried her best not to break down in front of me while she was driving although when I looked over at her, I could tell she had wiped her tears before I got in the car. We didn't say much. I didn't want to talk. We got home and the bag of goodies from my midwife was waiting on my doorstep. It consisted of calming teas, grape juice, sleeping pills and other things I don't recall. I took the sleeping pills upstairs, placed them on my nightstand which was on the right side of the bed, since I begged my husband to switch sides with me throughout my pregnancy. The right seemed more comfortable since he left his indentation there. I sat on the floor against a wall in my bedroom and stared off and my mind began to roam. My mother came up and joined me on my bedroom floor. I started to speak very calmly. I told her it just didn't feel real. Like how could this be happening to me? She began responding with soft listening words. My eyes began to well up with tears as all I could utter out was *Why? Why? Why?*

What did I do? Why would God do this to me? Why me? Did I do something wrong? I just don't understand. It's like He doesn't love me. By this point I'm hysterical. I'm saying things I never thought I'd hear fly out of my own mouth, especially about God. I always felt like I had a special relationship with God. All my life I've felt connected to Him and always able to hear the Holy Spirit. He's allowed me to endure many hardships throughout my life that I've grown through and learned from, but this was different. I felt betrayed. My mother couldn't help it anymore. She joined me in anguish and then she asked, "Can I hug you?" I said yes and she embraced me as if she was catching me from falling into a pit of fire. She held onto me the way I needed and we sobbed together. We both needed that hug.

Eventually I got up, wiped my tears, took a shower, and changed my clothes for bed. I took a sleeping pill and laid in bed looking ever so often at the time on my phone for when my husband's plane would be landing. He called me once he got off the plane and in his car to let me know he was on his way. I stayed up. I heard his car pull in and the lock sound from his car go off. I listened as he came through the door and greeted my mother. She told him I was upstairs. I saw his silhouette fill the dark room I was lying in and he came through the door. We made eye contact through the darkness and he then rushed over to embrace me tightly. He then got on his knees and placed his hand on my belly and laid his head in my lap for a while. He said, “I think I feel movement.” I said, “I know, I saw what looked like chest movement on the ultrasound and they told me it's called phantom movement, something that occurs after death but with no heartbeat the baby isn’t alive. I told him I had them check the heartbeat again and still nothing. He then held my hands and prayed for me, my health, my delivery, and our child. He finished and looked at me and said, “We have to have hope. It’s not over yet. God has the final say.”

At this point the moon was shining in some light through our window and I was able to clearly look him in his eyes. He truly meant what he said and believed it. The faith that I had earlier had honestly wavered but staring my husband in his eyes restored my faith so much, I had hope once again. He then asked me to go on a walk and we went outside and walked our neighborhood about three times, the cicadas filling the air with their loud noises in the trees. We talked about what I experienced before he arrived and we then devised a plan to believe our son was alive despite what anyone else said to us. After circling our neighborhood three times we got in the car and he just drove the late night, early morning streets. My sleeping pill finally kicked in and I got super drowsy and fell asleep. He woke me up when we got home and we got in the bed and rested.

The next morning my Mom woke up to check on us and asked if we were hungry. She picked up an order of food for us all from our favorite breakfast place five minutes from our house. While she was away my midwife called me to see if I decided to start my induction process at home or in a hospital. I chose to start at home. The birthing center I was seeing before all of this transpired called in a legal dosage of Cytotec that I could start at home to help ripen my cervix so it could open and help me to begin going into labor. At this point I was literally building a birthing plan I never wanted to have.

My mother got back with our food and I remember telling her, “I have hope today and I feel good. I have an appetite and I’m doing alright.” I was able to laugh and joke and carry on my day. I watched an old story about a miracle where a baby was delivered dead but came alive once the mother took hold of her. So I held on to that. I’ve never heard of a baby coming back to life but I knew if anyone could do it, God could if he wanted to.

Chapter 4:
The Road to Delivery

On Day 3, my midwife called to let me know that since I hadn't had any labor progression on my own, it was time to get to a hospital. I wasn't sure where to go. She told us to come to the birthing center. We packed our "hospital bag" and got in the car for an hour-long drive to the birthing center. The owner of the center, also a midwife, checked my cervix and administered a higher dosage of the induction meds vaginally. We also tried stimulating my breasts with my breast pump to get some contractions going but that didn't help either. Finally, she said firmly but as sympathetic as she could be, "You can not deliver your baby here. You will need to go to a hospital at this point." My original midwife finally arrived and tried to empathize with me. She shared her full detailed child loss story about her first child. But at that moment, I didn't want to relate. I was trying to hold on to hope again.

While they discussed the death of our child, when they left the room we continued to speak life because we knew they couldn't believe what we were believing for, which was a miracle. I still listened to all of their medical advice, though. They were kind enough to come up with a birthing plan with me to ensure I could have a peaceful delivery even though it would be in a hospital bed and not in a tub as I once dreamed of. For a moment I wondered, why did I even come here to the birthing center? Why would they have me come all the way here if they knew they couldn't really help me much? So I asked them, and their response was that it was just to get me out of the house so I could have some space to breathe and think in a different environment. Ok, I get that.

I pondered over where I would go to deliver and I finally settled on INOVA Alexandria. This was the hospital I was going to originally deliver at before I switched to a birthing center and I was familiar with them from a previous visit, the 25 week dehydration scare I had during my second trimester. The midwives called the hospital to inform them I was coming in that night and to let them know my current "situation" so they could prepare properly. Then, they handed me copies of my birthing plan and sent me on my way. We stopped for food first at a restaurant we go to frequently, Busboys and Poets. I wasn't hungry, but I knew I should probably eat something since I may be stuck in the hospital for a few days. I ordered my food while we were on the way there. We went inside to the bar to wait for our food to come out. I checked my food and it was completely wrong. I let the server know and she was very rude to me. I just burst into tears. I was already trying with everything inside of me to hold it together. I was already feeling like I was in limbo, sort of lost in my current reality. I didn't even have the strength to speak to her to fix my order. I just looked at my husband and asked if he would get it fixed for me. Then the bartender came up and she saw I was pregnant and waiting on my food. "When are you due?" she asked. "I'm currently going through induction," I told her. She went on to say she was also induced just a few months ago and gave birth to her baby. She had no idea the trauma I'd endured thus far and that I was hoping and praying I, too would see my child alive after birth. My food came out and we left for the hospital. I barely ate.

When we arrived we had to go through the normal check-in process. As we were processing, reality hit me and everything just felt so crazy to me like, "Wow, I'm really in the hospital right now and I have no idea what's about to happen next." I get up to the labor and delivery hall and to my room. It was very tiny. I get undressed and into the hospital gown. Nurse Kendra walked into the room and began to hook me up to IVs and monitors. She was honestly so delightful to have around. There was something special about her spirit that was so genuine, sweet, and relatable. She treated me like a person and not just another patient. She was thorough and careful. This was in May of 2021 and COVID rules were in place so I was only allowed one visitor. They allowed my mother to come in as well during the duration of my stay by the grace of God, considering the circumstances. I was surrounded by the two people who know me best and always show me unrelenting love and support. I needed that. They actually had to share a hard, barely twin-size bed in a sometimes cold room, but they thugged it out on my behalf. We were all three in this together, every step of the way.

On Day 4 of induction there wasn't much progress at all. I was finally at about 2cm dilated when the shifts changed. On this day I met a new nurse, a nurse who seemed like she knew what she was doing and who would actually care for me. She tried to be "relatable" by commenting on things she assumed my Mom, husband or myself might like based on the show we were watching at the time: Fresh Prince. She continued administering pain-relief drugs, checking my cervix, and inserting induction meds at the appropriate time. Throughout her shift I kept asking her if she could ask the doctor to come in to see me. I wanted to go over my plan with him and hear his thoughts on how to get this process in more of a progression. I mean we were on day 4 at this point. She kept saying, "He's going to come," but he never showed. I understand doctors are busy and there are many other patients to care for, but dang. My life felt like it was hanging in the balance. He could've popped in for 2 minutes or so just to say "Hello, I'll be with you soon" or to give his recommendations.

This wasn't a light case to handle. I potentially had a lifeless child deteriorating in my body. Trust me, I still held on to hope but without saying anything to my Mom or husband I also could feel him inside of me, but it wasn't the same. He felt limp inside my womb by this point.

Fast forward to the doctor having maybe an hour left on his shift, he came in after my mother went out to try to find someone above this nurse of mine. Let's say her name was Susanna, the day 4 daytime shift nurse. The doctor finally came, strolling in nonchalantly. Susanna followed behind him and she went from me looking at her as sweet Susanna to, *who the hell does she think she is?* Susanna completely switched up on me. The doctor had zero ounces of compassion for my situation. No "sorry it took so long" or "I'm sorry you are having to deal with this." I know that would've been a courtesy as he's really only required to do his actual job, but he didn't even seem to want to do that. That was the straw that broke the camel's back for me. When I asked him what can be done to speed this up since we were about to go into a 5-day induction he said, "I don't have all the answers. What do you want me to do? Give you a C-section?" I said, "No, if that's not necessary, I don't want that." He says, "Well, that's the quickest way to get the baby out." I respond, "Well, it doesn't seem like you're trying to really help and it sounds like you're just throwing whatever out at me as advice. I don't feel safe." Then here comes Susanna's behind jumping in to defend Doctor Nonchalant. You would've thought they were dating or something as Doctor Nonchalant looks at her for approval, nodding his head like "look at my woman coming to my rescue." They both sounded looney tunes in my opinion. I had to tell Susanna, "No offense but you are not the doctor and I was not talking to you." I got so fed up I told them I may need to leave and go somewhere else. He said, "I understand. But if you want a C-section, let me know."

I could not believe how careless this doctor seemed. I looked around at my husband and Mom and I think they were in shock because they looked stunned and didn't know what to say. My husband finally asked the nurse and doctor to leave the room to give us time to think. I was heated, blood boiling with fury. It really felt like I was being treated so carelessly by this doctor because I was Black. Maybe this wasn't the case and he treated all of his patients this way, but I couldn't help but to feel my black maternal body was being neglected from proper care just as I've read and heard happens to a lot of our women. Here I was experiencing some form of it, having to advocate for my health even though I didn't have all the answers and all the knowledge. I wished my midwife was there at that point. I contacted her and let her know what was happening but she got back to me later than I needed because she was helping with another birth at the time I reached out. So this decision to stay or go was on me and God.

My mom called around to a family nurse she knew. My husband asked me questions and then I just sat quietly and prayed in my head for answers and stared at the wall for what felt like eternity but in all actuality it was probably about 30-45 minutes. While staring at the wall I contemplated decisions I could make and their outcomes. I thought, well I could leave and start this process all over at a different hospital as my midwife suggested, and then I thought that may get confusing and become more stressful. I could leave and go home and let my body just do what it needs to do, even if that means something happens to me, or I could stay and continue the process I started here. I finally asked my mother to check with the front desk to see when this particular doctor and nurse would be changing shifts and when they'd be back. She found out they were leaving soon and the night shift was about to rotate in. Nurse Susanna wouldn't be back in the morning but Doctor Nonchalant would be back the next afternoon. I chose to stay and requested that Nurse Kendra come back in when she returned to work.

The shifts changed and this Middle-Eastern, no-nonsense powerhouse named Dr. Salgada strolled in playing zero games. She came in, greeted me, showed great sympathy for my current experience, read through my birth plan, and came up with a new safe induction plan to speed things along. Y'all Nurse Susanna was still there for another 30 minutes to an hour and Dr. Salgada whipped her into shape right in front of me. She was like, "Why aren't you doing what I asked when I ask? I need you to do this and that for her right now."

Needless to say I never had to explain what I currently experienced with her to anyone but God knew. Susanna never peeped another careless word. You could tell she knew she couldn't play any games under the leadership of my girl Dr. Salgada. I knew I was in the right hands at this point and all three of us, my mom, husband, and myself prayed that I would go into labor under her and Nurse Kendra's care. And I did. Right at that next nurse shift change.

At about 12:45am I woke up from a deep slumber. I looked around and both my Mom and husband were knocked out. I started feeling what seemed like a sudden jolt of lightning, but it didn't hurt. It was just enough of a sensation to know I needed to call the nurse in because I had never felt that before. As the sensation passed, she came in and started looking at the monitor and readjusting the contraction bands around my belly. While she was in the room, I felt my water break. It felt like someone burst a pipe in my vagina but this didn't hurt either, just more so surprising. Then, in a matter of seconds, things started to move super fast. I started to feel like I had to throw up and take a dump at the same time. So I got out of bed and by the time I made it to the toilet I also felt a strong lightning feeling pierce through my body. I yelled out in anguish for my husband to get up and come into the bathroom with me. Nurse Kendra turned on all the lights and started informing the doctor and setting up.

My husband stood there and rubbed my back and held my hand as I threw up in the trash can and defecated in the toilet. He's a real one for sure. I'm quite sure it smelled horrific in there. I felt like I couldn't move every time a new contraction came on. I yelled out, "PLEASE give me that epidural now!" The nurse stood at the door to ensure my needs were taken care of. She then called for the anesthesiologist to come to my room. My husband said I kept saying under my breath, "I should've got it sooner, I should've got it sooner." I finally mustered up the strength to get off the toilet knowing I couldn't stay there, especially if I expected an epidural to be administered. Once a contraction passed, I got up and headed over to the bed. I'm in complete agony at this point and I knew it was on like Donkey Kong. This was it. I was literally about to push this baby out of my body.

Chapter 5: The Birth of Our Son

Now the anesthesiologist comes in and I promise she reminded me of Ms. Frizzle from *The Magic School Bus* in the best way possible. She had the most cheerful, positive attitude and amazing energy as she waltzed in the room. I could tell she loved her job and was probably really good at it. Now I will say she was taking way too long to explain this process to me with me wincing in pain. She was very thorough but to be honest, I was in so much pain I just wanted her to get on with it. I braced through the next wave of contractions that were so strong I wanted to scream and do anything but sit still. I squeezed my husband's hand so tight as the needle that I opted not to see beforehand pierced through my back and into my spine to distribute the epidural into my body. A few moments later, my lower body was completely numb, and I could no longer feel the strength of those contractions. I was smiling again. I remember saying,

"I'm so glad I got these drugs, what was I thinking before?" Everyone burst out into laughter and I turned into a comedian for a few minutes. I was so relieved and thankful for whoever invented the epidural at that moment.

Now my legs felt like they weighed a ton and I couldn't move them without assistance nor was I allowed to walk until after birth and after the epidural had worn off completely. I also experienced intense body chills. I couldn't stop shaking no matter how many blankets they threw on me. (Well they didn't literally throw them on me, but you know what I mean). Apparently body chills are one of the side effects from receiving an epidural, and I was grateful that was the only thing I had to deal with after getting one. I'd heard tons of horror stories about side effects after getting an epidural and even of numerous risks during the administration of it. For me, I made a conscious decision for myself to get one, especially because I knew I may not reap the reward of a living, crying baby that I could say the pain was worth enduring. To be honest, even if this were a normal experience the intensity of those induction labor pains were so intense so quickly, I probably would have still asked for an epidural. I believe you should always be aware of all risk factors and make a conscious decision for yourself once you are thoroughly educated.

So anyways, I'm now lying in the hospital bed, shivering underneath a pile of blankets and not even realizing I'm contracting. As I'm cracking jokes with my mom and husband, the nurse comes in, looks at the monitor and goes, "Can you feel that?" I said, "Feel what? She said, "Oh, this epidural is really working for you." She then put my legs in stirrups and as soon as she looked at my vagina she said, "Oh my goodness, his head is right there. It's time for you to start pushing!" She swiftly starts setting everything up for labor and calls the doctor to come in. For about the first 30 minutes of pushing the nurse was the only medical professional in the room. She allowed me to try to labor in any position I felt comfortable in. I started by leaning against a bar to try to push in a squat position and then by lying on my left side, but neither of these positions were working for me to progress my labor. In hindsight, I just may not have been pushing right, but who knows. I never got a chance to take child birthing classes as I had planned to take in my 36th week with my midwife but of course we know I didn't make it there. I really didn't know what I was doing. I'd seen YouTube videos but all of that went out the window.

After some time the doctor came in and she began to coach me through. I couldn't feel the contractions at all at this point, so my body had no natural response to know when it was time. My husband had a gospel playlist on rotation in the background and the lights were very dim, only shining on the doctor, the nurse, and my vagina. I remember feeling super at peace and calm while pushing. I was fully present and trusting my body to push out our baby. I really feel like God surrounded the room with a spiritual calmness, like a realm of protection. At one point the doctor said, "Ok, big push!" and nothing happened. Then she said, "If you can't do this, I will have to cut you." I firmly told her, "NO! I got this!" As tired as I was, we progressed through. I knew I had to activate the last bit of energy and all my might to get my body to push this baby through my canal, and I did. He finally came out.

My husband looked down at our first born child, then looked at me and shook his head no. I knew that any hope we had left of him possibly being a miracle and crying or even looking the least bit alive had finally come to an end. He was actually gone, and I was not going to experience the miracle I thought I would. God did not grant me my desire and I had to be ok with that. They asked if I wanted to hold him but my husband said he didn't think that I should. The doctor said our son looked dehydrated and limp from being dead in my womb for so many days, so some parts of him may not look as they should. I ultimately decided not to hold him. My husband said, "I think that's for the best. I wouldn't want you to replay his image this way in your mind over and over. It's going to be hard enough." He was right. He knew me. Mentally I can hold on to so much. I do believe holding him in that way would have shattered me into more pieces than I already was about to endure. My mother didn't look up close at him either – it was too hard. But my husband saw it all. He watched our son enter the world without life in his body. He saw him up close and protected us all mentally and bore the weight of it all on himself. This was an image that later he had to battle with over and over and over again. We will get to that in just a few though.

I asked the doctors to still place him in the hospital bassinet under the light across the room. I stared at my son from across the room, examining the length of his body, his skin, his hair, and the features I could make out from across the room. I couldn't believe this long, almost 5-pound child was inside of me. I was still amazed that I grew such a beautiful human. Oddly enough, I did not cry. None of us did. We just stared at him from afar and took in the beauty of what was created.

After a while, the team came back in to give me options, paperwork, and to talk about next steps. They even asked if I wanted pictures. I had them swaddle him in blankets in a unique way to leave out parts of his body like his hands, feet, and nose. They brought him back to the room and allowed my husband and I some time to pray over our child's spirit and release him back to God. We decided this was enough for us. We knew if we couldn't physically have his spirit that possesses a soul living in his body here on earth, that him being with God was the very best place. We knew he was very well taken care of as a baby angel with our other loved ones who had transitioned over. This was the first time I cried while in the hospital. It was very hard to say goodbye. You never imagine sending your child, your first born, your baby to heaven as soon as they touch earth but this was our reality. I held his little hands one last time, told him we loved him and sent his spirit off to glory. They rolled him out of the room.

They asked if we wanted to have a funeral, if we wanted pictures (again), and a whole list of other things right away. So many decisions that we had to make right then and there. It was all so overwhelming. We asked them to just give us a moment. We ultimately decided against a funeral service because we felt we had done all we needed to as his parents by returning his spirit back over to God after praying for him. That is what was right for us. We needed to start our healing process. Let's not forget I still had to go through all things postpartum every mother goes through after giving birth. I just didn't have a child to take home and tend to. After the nurse did her final checks on me, pressing down on my abdomen to release anything else that needed to come out, and me finally urinating on my own after the epidural completely wore off, I was free to go home. I didn't even go to the postpartum recovery hall, so when I went to the bathroom I could hear another mother hooked up to the monitor through the wall listening to her baby's heartbeat and I remember thinking, "Wow, that must be nice." We all gathered up our belongings. My mother left out first. Unbeknownst to me she had gone to the nurses' desk to ask if they would take very specific pictures of the baby, like his hands and feet and such, and put them away for me in case I ever called back and changed my mind. I'm so glad she did that because a few days later I wished I had them and my mom was able to tell me they were already taken and waiting for me.

After my husband and I took our last sweep of this small hospital room we lived in for the last three days, we both agreed that as soon as I was healed up, at about 7 weeks, we would need to get out of town and go somewhere to clear our heads and relax. The nurse wheeled me out of the room while my husband went to pull the car around. I was holding on to a keepsake box with a lock of his hair and other memorable items of his, and a box with his footprints. As I was being rolled down the hall my ears were filled with healthy baby heartbeats from other rooms. I went numb. They rolled me outside and my husband helped me get in the car. I looked back at no car seat but just a place to rest his boxes. My husband and I looked at each other and broke down into tears. It was as if every emotion came out at once. We didn't speak a word, we just wept. It was like a tide had rushed in from the deepest part of the ocean and overtook our bodies. This is when it hit us that this is actually real and we will have to exist in the world without the child that we thought we would have. Not only that, but it just felt so unfair to roll out from giving birth yet have absolutely no child to bring home and care for. I do believe this is truly when stages of grief began for the both of us and we handled it very differently.

We were grieving the loss of our son on the same day – a Thursday – that we were supposed to have our second baby shower. Everything was set and ready to go.

Then I gave birth to my stillborn son that morning. The baby shower was supposed to happen that afternoon and by the time I left the hospital people were already showing up. But my friend who graciously planned everything had just found out that morning what we were going through and she had to cancel the entire event and all the vendors. Guests were sent home due to the news of us losing our son.

I felt completely numb. Like I really had no feelings towards it. Of course I felt bad that she would lose out on money and hoped due to the circumstance she'd recoup back every dollar spent but I didn't have the capacity to worry about the shower because what had just happened was so monumental, so earth-shaking. Yet I felt so still . . . still in the world after birthing my stillborn son just a few hours ago. Everything just, paused.

Chapter 6: The Process of Grieving

We listened to music as we continued down the road and I just kept weeping. My husband stopped to pick me up some food and on our journey home from the hospital. My mother had cleaned our house before coming to the hospital to join us, so it was nice to come back to a clean house after what we had just experienced that morning.

I remember sitting on the couch just to sort of recollect. My husband said his parents were about to stop by. I honestly didn't feel like having company at the time. I was sitting on the couch wrapped in a blanket and hospital diaper, bleeding out of my vagina. I literally just gave birth a few hours ago. I'm vulnerable in every way. At the time I knew he probably could use the presence of his parents, as we'd had the comfort of my mother this entire time, so I didn't say anything. I always make a point to prioritize his well-being and state of mind too. He is my husband.

I put on a brave face as they came through the door to sit with us. After a while I said goodbye to them and kindly went upstairs to change my hospital undies and lie down. I was exhausted. I hadn't had decent sleep in days and at that point I had been up a complete 12 hours and went through the Olympic sport of giving birth within those 12 hours. My body was calling for my bed.

After sleeping for some time, I woke up much later in the evening and mustered up the energy to take a visit. My friend Kelli came over, the one that planned the DC shower and we sat in her car and talked for a few hours. Well actually, I talked for a few hours and she just listened. She allowed me space to cry, express myself and how I felt. Friend to friend. Mother to mother. I needed that. I honestly never stopped talking as the days went by. Though I appreciated my solitude, I needed space to speak. My mother turned what was supposed to be a weekend visit into a two month visit. She was allowed time off from work to grieve with us. I am so grateful she was with us. I needed her deeply.

Each morning I woke up to a new stage of grief that I never planned to encounter. I read that there are five stages of grief: Denial, Anger, Bargaining, Depression, and Acceptance. I can't say that I experienced them all but I did get hit with a few for different lengths of time. Denial didn't live in my orbit beyond just thinking at one point, "Wow. I can't believe this really happened to me. This is really my story. I really have a child in heaven that I gave birth to. Like I really just went through a lot." I was more so in a state of shock for a moment but it was too real for me to be in denial.

I do however remember waking up one day and I was so angry. I was angry with God. Not enough to turn my back on him completely, but I was furious enough that I wasn't afraid to say how angry he made me feel out loud. I remember telling my Mom how mad I was and how I didn't feel like I could trust Him. Like, why would he send a whole prophet my way to tell me I was pregnant, to pray with me, to tell me about personality traits my son would have, etc., just to rip it all away? Like why would He do all that? I was so confused. All she could do was listen and allow me space to speak. She didn't try to make sense of it but my mother still stood on God's word and shared His love through her presence. I don't know how she does it. Well I guess she doesn't try – God's love just naturally shines through her. But I was still angry with God for an entire day.

Then it moved to bargaining. I kept trying to find answers. I filmed a short film during my first trimester of being pregnant with my son, when I was about eight weeks along. In the short film I played the main character, which happened to be a mother who lost her child. So I called the director and asked her if that story was personal to her. She said no, but it was a story she wanted to tell. I kept looking for a correlation, someone with a similar story, and just a reason to make sense of it all. I think I needed to feel understood, or just to have some sort of justification. Maybe both.

Eventually, my Mom showed me an episode of *Black Love* on the OWN Network. It was when Felicia and Karega Bailey shared their story of going through child loss. They also had a stillbirth far along, just like me. Actually, further along than I was, and for the first time I felt extremely understood and not alone. I didn't know anyone around me who had been through anything like this specifically. I had people tell me about their miscarriages which is also extremely sad and I myself have never experienced a loss in that aspect, but it just didn't resonate with the type of loss I experienced. It wasn't the same for me. I needed to hear from someone with a story extremely similar to mine and within the same time frame. It just so happened that their story was.

I knew right away I wanted to reach out to Felicia on social media and that's just what I did. She responded and it was nice to finally not feel alone and to have someone who had been on this journey of motherhood I had just started. Plus, she'd already had her second child. She was exactly who I needed to hear from. She gave me hope and I appreciated her kindness in choosing to hold space for me and my heavenly little one. I eventually also spoke to another young lady who had experienced a stillbirth and a miscarriage. Her perspective on loss was relatable for me but it was also unique to hear how she processed both losses the same. I realized no one grieves identically.

Hearing the inner details of both of these ladies' processes and the countless women I started reading about and listening to via YouTube and Instagram prompted me to release the idea that my grief journey had to look similar to theirs. I thought at one point there was a right or wrong way to process this part of my story, but there wasn't. This was my journey for a reason. The more I sought community, the more I was able to move forward, one foot in front of the other.

There is something powerful about understanding you are not alone in what you're going through or that you're not the only one who experienced it. Sometimes life has a way of making you feel like an anomaly, and while that in itself is isolating and lonely, maybe sometimes even feeling that way has value and is necessary. We're only human, right? We are absolutely allowed the space to feel this way but from my experience it's not ok to *stay* in the staleness of that type of darkness. Looking towards the light and deciding to eventually put one foot in front of the other at some point despite how tough it is to carry will do wonders for your soul when you are ready.

I personally believe my healing process was largely due to the people God allowed to show up for me, coupled with me still acknowledging him. I still prayed even though I didn't always feel that He was hearing me or talking to me at the time, and I spent time with God even though I felt I had nothing to say, I also went to therapy. It helped. It all helped.

One thing to add, and this is vital and I try not to think about this that often because I blamed myself for a while, even though I know that this definitely has no effect on what happened. I believe that what happened was in God's plan all along, I couldn't have done anything to stop it.

But when my husband was away, we had a conversation the night before. We got into an argument and I asked him to come back because I was angry that he was going out and having fun even though we were in the middle of a pandemic and he could've brought COVID-19 back home to me. My hormones were all over the place. We got into a really bad argument and I told him he just needed to come home.

I went to sleep really angry and then I woke up feeling very eerie, not about the conversation I had with my husband, but about how I was feeling in my body. My son wasn't responding. And I went all day with that same eerie feeling. And I wondered, "Did I cause myself too much stress?" And I never wanted to say this out loud to too many people because I never wanted to feel judged. I feel like I would be remiss if I didn't say this. I don't blame myself anymore but I was very conscious the second time around to never be stressed. People are stressed all the time throughout pregnancy. It's never good. This was a part of God's plan for whatever reason, and it's a part of my story.

I didn't understand it all but I knew one thing for sure: there was no way God would allow me to go through something of this magnitude for no reason. I started feeling like I could relate to his servant Job in the Bible. Job lost so much more but this was my Job moment in my life. I've always thought Job's story was so extreme but his faith was crazy strong even when he questioned God at one point. It showed his humanity and made his trials relatable to all of us reading his story.

I had read Job's story again a few months before I lost my son, maybe even a year before when I was still going through bodily health challenges. It made me feel then that I, too, could have enough faith to believe in the Lord despite what my situation currently looked like. At the time that was the hardest thing I ever had to deal with, but little did I know God had more to allow me to endure. This was now the hardest experience I ever had to go through. Losing my son. My first born child. I didn't go read Job's story again; it just came back to my mind one day during my healing process. I remember saying something to the effect of, "Oh, ok. Now I see what this is, God. You're testing my faith in a major way just like you did your servant Job. You want to see if I'll still believe and trust in you despite what it all looks like." I'm pretty sure I said out loud, "I still trust you."

I was maturing in my faith. My journey with God was changing and it honestly didn't feel good or seem fair at all. Just as one of Kirk Franklin's songs, "Just For Me" says:

But trusting in your timing is not easy

And what I want is not always what I need

Somewhere I forgot

You are God and I am not

I see, if I could speak honestly

It don't feel good

But growing never does

It don't seem fair

For you to call this love

But if necessary pain

Is the ingredient for change

Even when life may be bittersweet

It's working just for me.

Songs like this and countless other songs that were uplifting eventually helped open my spirit back up to hope. Some songs weren't even necessarily Gospel but still brought me joy. Music was a huge part of my healing journey. My husband and I listened to feel-good music daily all throughout the house.

While I was in therapy my therapist mentioned this seemed like a new test of faith for me, which I agreed with, but she also said some things will have no explanation. Some things just happen and are a part of life. I understood what she was saying and this may be the case for some instances. But I knew I couldn't agree with this in totality. For me, it just didn't make sense. Something had to come out of this: growth, stronger faith, encouragement for others at some point, a learned lesson or lessons, this book. Something.

But I did learn it wasn't healthy for me to get stuck in the obsession of finding some concrete answer other than knowing for sure this had to be a test of faith. Honestly that was something, even if that was all it was for. I learned a lot about myself through my healing journey and my therapist helped me realize I had a lot of maturing to do mentally that I wasn't aware of before this all happened. I viewed certain aspects of God and my life as a fantasy or a fairytale. I was holding onto ideologies and thought processes from my childhood and expecting things to work out just as I thought or saw them come to pass as a child. The reality is that as we grow up we evolve, and so does our relationship with God. It was time for me to step into a new level of faith and understand God in a new way, which was uncomfortable for me. It made my faith seem less exciting because it was so hard. Like tough love. God was there but it was different. I was expanding and changing. I formed new thought processes and ways of responding to situations.

Even now I may veer to prudent thinking, only seeing what's in front of me, and I forget I can still be optimistic. The difference as I'm still healing and growing is that I give myself so much more grace now. I allow myself to feel and think those thoughts and then allow myself to cast them away and usher in hope and exercise my faith because I do still believe he's in the blessing business. Often times, my husband will snap me out of negative thinking quickly with some sort of positive reinforcement. I'm so grateful his faith increased in a way that he's the one gathering me and encouraging me to still believe when I detour down negativity lane. Again, I'm human. A continuous work in progress. But aren't we all?

Chapter 7: The Fourth Trimester

The time my husband and I shared after returning home to grieve and heal was beautiful and unique. In the beginning he was my tree that I leaned on and he willingly assumed that role. He catered to my needs and allowed space for me to heal emotionally. We talked about our son and how we felt almost everyday, especially when we'd go outside and sit on our patio late at night. Just the two of us, staring at the stars, candles lit, listening to music and just being present. Sometimes those nights would consist of tears and some nights they didn't. He also allowed me space to get the comfort I needed from my mother without feeling like he wasn't needed because he was. I only mention this because my husband loves to do things for me and I love watching and allowing him to do them. Mom allowed him to have a good break those first six weeks. She was cooking, cleaning, and staying in the house a lot with me during the day. My husband needed that space and time to leave the house. He was able to go play golf with his brothers or Dad, meet up with mutual friends who stepped in and started taking him to watch games and out to eat to get him out the house. He was able to go to the gym and clear his mind. None of this bothered me because I knew what he needed since we always communicated. He needed to be able to stay active and get out of the house. If my mother hadn't been with me during this time he would've stayed cooped up with me all day, so I believe it was best this way. It allowed us both time to breathe.

I knew him staying in the house only made him sadder. He was processing differently. I wanted him to go to therapy as well because I knew the magnitude of all of this would hit him suddenly later. In fact I remember saying, "Babe, you have to deal with this and talk it out with a specialist, someone who can help you process your feelings further. You keep saying you're fine but it's going to chase you down and eat you alive later." Now I didn't have to say it was going to eat him alive later but I knew him. He responded, "Well, let it." I knew I couldn't force his process or expect it to look like mine. He only talked about it with me but I knew there was so much more to uncover. He saw our child come out of my birth canal lifeless. That's an image you can't erase. He took on the weight of seeing what I couldn't see in order to protect my mental health.

What I didn't realize is that I actually may have been the only person he needed to speak to. Little by little, he revealed more of his feelings and hangups. He shared with me how helpless he felt seeing our child coming into this world with his soul already gone, knowing there was absolutely nothing he could do about it. Not to mention our child looked just like him, which he told me because he got a really good look at him. Our son was his Junior, a name he preserved just for him. Through therapy I was learning to become a better communicator and listener. He didn't need me to fix anything, he just needed me to be there to listen and support him.

♦♦♦

During my postpartum recovery time my friend Alicia flew in at the drop of a hat to stay with me for a few days while I was still in my initial six-week postpartum recovery. It was so nice to just have company. My cousins Sidney and Paris came by to spend time with me and my best friend Alexis flew in to be with me as well. She even helped fill spaces in my home with new things to make it feel better to sit in. Also during this six week period my mom finally returned home. My friend Reese came over often to sit, bring food, and check on us both. A few other friends came over for a quick chat or to drop off food as well.

Everyone's presence and support was needed in the exact time frame that they were given to bless my space in the way that they did. Not to mention the countless phone calls from those who couldn't physically be with me meant so much. But I wanted more physical support for my husband. He got some, but I knew he needed more.

When I was seven weeks postpartum, me and Devon went to Puerto Rico, the trip we planned the first week after leaving the hospital. We knew we would need it and we did. It was right on time.

I honestly felt very uncomfortable in my body. I was wearing real clothes for the first time since I gave birth and my body was not at all where it was pre-pregnancy. Now I had to learn how to live in my new body and give myself grace in an area I never knew I'd struggle in. I felt so awkward in this new body but my husband kept telling me how beautiful I was, and he loved on every new inch. Can I just say thank God for a partner who loves me for me, empowers me, and makes me feel so beautiful even when I didn't?! Man I love that man. I know y'all didn't ask for all the gushiness so I will spare you because I could really go there, okay?! But back to the story. This trip we took was so fun and relaxing. We didn't do too much besides sit by the water, eat, and explore. That's all we needed, though – just to be away and with each other.

On our last day there, my husband got a phone call that his Aunt had passed away from cancer. This was extremely tough to hear. We talked through it and I knew this was yet another added layer to the grief he was already experiencing with losing his son. I'm so glad he got to see her and spend time with her before we left. This was the Aunt he joked and laughed with the most. She had such a fun personality. They were so fun to watch together and she is truly missed. When we found out, we knew that when we got back home we would be going to a funeral in just a few days. Within 6-7 weeks my husband had lost his first son, his namesake, and one of his favorite Aunts. It was now my turn to be his tree to lean on.

I checked in on his mental health and through my own time in therapy I learned techniques on how to allow him his space to speak, how to listen when he wanted to talk, and how to inquire in a way of support instead of just trying to solve the problem the way I did before. I learned through our separate grief journeys better ways to communicate and how to just simply be there. It's healthy to ask direct and "hard" questions like, "I notice you are really quiet. Are you thinking about our son?" I made a point to never shy away from exactly what was in front of us. If you dance around situations and avoid hard or uncomfortable conversations through hardships or healing journeys I feel you miss a beautiful opportunity to strengthen your bond with your partner and your level of communication. They may not answer you right away and sometimes they have a lot to say while other times they don't, but still hold the space. Everyone else around you is probably trying to avoid asking about things because they assume it's too hard for you to talk about but in reality, it's the opposite. You need to talk about it (if you're ready). As your loved one's partner in life, you are the one they can come to and let it all out with, the one with whom they feel safe to share. This creates an even more magnetic bond between the two of you. That's what it did for my marriage.

About two months after we lost our son and after his Aunt passed, everything finally came tumbling down on him. While it was still tough to process for me, I had been dealing with it and was in the upswing of my healing journey. To see my husband finally process his grief was very difficult for me to watch. It made me so sad to see him so torn, but I knew it was my turn to continue to be his tree to lean on and to be a little stronger for him, just as he was for me those first two months when I needed to talk it out frequently and was crying nonstop.

I watched him mostly sit in silence with not very much to say. He didn't really want to go anywhere anymore and he started taking notice of who was checking on him, who was really there for him. I knew he was feeling isolated, so I sat with him. We watched things that made us laugh, like this Progressive commercial that seemed to play all the time. It was so hilarious to me that even if we weren't watching a funny show or movie, that commercial always popped up right on time to give us a break of genuine soul-filling laughter. We started watching a competition style series that was interesting to talk about, and a nice distraction. Sometimes he didn't want to talk, and sometimes he said he was fine when I knew he was not. I kept checking in. I kept asking him direct questions, not annoyingly but just to let him know, "Hey, it's safe to speak." Eventually he shared more and more and I listened. I thought of creative ways to cheer him up, like dancing with him and initiating fun stuff that he enjoys, like being active. I tried things to make him feel super thought of and important so he knew I was doing it just for him. I was intentional with this because I've seen my husband pour back into others selflessly , all the time, but I know he doesn't always get the same in return. As his wife I knew he needed that special attention and though I try to always be cognizant of this and give him that, I knew he needed extra, even from me.

One Saturday morning, I told him not to make plans and to dress comfortably for an outside activity. I surprised him with a local hiking adventure, something we did once before in Arizona when we hiked up a mountain, and he really enjoyed it. I found a nice trail about 20-30 minutes away and we went for it. Getting him outside amongst nature's wonders, being active, and having great energy made our hike so fun and it definitely cheered him up. I saw his light start to shine bright again. He was laughing and joking around like his usual self. Granted, I know one day doesn't fix everything . . . or can it? I'm not sure, but what matters is it made a difference along his healing journey. I could tell. Maybe because it was something fun in a place we had never been before together.

After that, we started going to the gym together more. He started saying things like, “I got my best friend back” and, “We can do stuff together again.” I knew what this was. He needed to talk and process but he also needed to be active and consistently do things. Being predominantly idle was not healthy for him mentally. Although when we first lost our son he was trying to remain active and continuously move, when the heaviness of it all started to weigh down more than he could bear, he sat idle. He just needed a reason, support, and encouragement to get up and keep placing one foot in front of the other.

We even arranged for one of his good friends to fly down to spend time with him. He was able to get some guy time in with him and another local friend that came over and I was so glad to see this. There was also an increase in communication from a few other guy friends who became closer to him through this time. My husband needed this. He needed to feel thought of, checked on, and supported by others as well. He needed community just as I did. It helped so much! I also continued praying for him because I desperately wanted my husband to heal forward and beautifully, and he did. We both continue to. Losing our son did not drive us apart. It brought us closer. It strengthened our marriage in a way that let us know we'll always have each other's back. We learned so much. We lean on each other and know how to exchange support levels when needed. I believe that without communication you don't have very much of a foundation to stand on in marriage or within a committed relationship. We talk about everything and we don't allow ourselves to shy away from hard topics. We even pray together more. When we're making big decisions, our first thought for each other is, "Did you pray about that?" or, "Ok, let's pray about it." I'm grateful God kept us. Thank you Lord!

Because I was now on an upswing, I was ready to start working again. My husband held it down himself throughout our pregnancy and my healing process. Although he never asked me to get back to work, I wanted to. I wanted to help take some of that load off of him. I knew I could work on my acting career and work at the same time and that is what I did. I believe the year I wasn't working was more of God's way of allowing me to learn to trust my husband to lead us. God knew my insecurities with not having much control financially. I was so used to always working and never wanting to feel broke because I'd been there before and it's not a good feeling. So I went from making almost six figures a year to nothing but unemployment and some money from selling shirts and mugs through my Etsy shop while I was pregnant, as I also had to pause my acting career. I learned that my husband was way better at managing bills than me, and I was a better saver. We learned our strengths with our finances. He was able to see exactly what I had and I could see what he had. We no longer kept our finances hidden. We shared everything.

I say all this to say I always believe God has a purpose in what He does, even when He takes things away from us. Now when I started working again I knew not to be selfish, I knew how to share our money as I watched my husband so graciously never be selfish with his. It was always "ours." I even learned how to manage money better and God opened doors for increase.

♦♦♦

During my healing process music was a huge factor as I mentioned before. My friend Alicia introduced an affirmation album to me by an artist named Toni Jones. She has this song called "Energy Budget" that I bumped every single day from the moment I heard it. This became a part of my routine as I started re-entering the world. I say re-entering because I started living more – going out in public for fun to the places I once visited with my pregnant belly. Some of the workers that I saw often in places I frequented began asking, "How's the baby? I see you had him." Here is when I began to carve out the answer I felt comfortable giving them and that was the truth. Not that I owed it to them but I owed it to me. To live in my truth unabashedly. This is my story. My answer often made others feel uncomfortable but it wasn't my job to soothe them. I noticed I was becoming a stronger version of myself even with the tender parts of me that still existed. My husband and I started dating each other more. We went out a lot! We mostly went out to eat and made it a goal to show up to functions our friends invited us to so that we could get dressed up and get out the house.

I finally got a new job and got back to acting. I was auditioning a lot again. I started juicing, detoxing, and working out consistently and lost about 30 pounds. I started creating content again. I started going out to eat with my friend Reese who lives here. She has been absolutely supportive throughout my healing journey and never shied away from asking me deep questions and checking on me mentally. I appreciated that. I was able to fit back into my clothes pre-pregnancy and I realized that focusing on my health and loving myself more was also a huge shift on the upswing of my healing journey. I felt more confident and I was ready for what was next.

Chapter 8: The Rainbow

It had been about 4.5 months since the loss of my son. I was about 6-8 pounds shy of my pre-pregnancy weight and I got a call from my Godmother. She said, "I was praying for you and I heard God say, "It's time." I said, "It's time for what?" She said, "I don't know, maybe it's time for you to be consistent with content creation and building a platform." I said, "Yeah, maybe you're right . . ." but I knew that wasn't it. When she said it, I immediately thought of a child. Then my other Godmother called me a few days later and asked me if I was pregnant because she had a dream I was in the hospital and came running up to her to say I just had a little girl. I simply told her, "Actually, I don't know if I'm pregnant or not." There was a possibility, I'm not going to lie. My husband and I were definitely having fun in the bedroom and there was this one time where . . . well, I'll spare you the details.

So I actually decided to take a test before my missed period. In fact I took three. I used Clearblue®

Digital and FIRST RESPONSE™. I had four sticks total but after three came back positive I didn't bother with the fourth. It was October at this point. I was overjoyed and recorded myself looking at my results because I knew I wanted to remember this moment and look back, especially if I was indeed pregnant.

Once again I thought of a way to share the news with my husband before he got home from work. This time instead of a silly TikTok dance reveal, I put two of the pee sticks in a small to-go box and placed some ginger at the bottom to give it some weight. When he got home I told him I picked him up some food earlier. He opened the box and started laughing. He then asked if we were having twins since there were two tests in the box. (Silly rabbit, tricks are for kids). I said no to the twins but honestly, who knew? I hadn't had an ultrasound yet. He was so happy and we shared another one of those long hugs with three sweet kisses, just like before. A few days later I had an appointment with my primary care doctor to further confirm the test so that I could make an OB appointment. My results came back negative. My primary care doctor said after them testing my urine my results were definitely negative. I told her about my positive at-home tests and she said it could have been a false read, but we'll draw your blood and send that in. Blood tests tend to be more accurate.

I got back in my car and I didn't cry but I was a wee bit disappointed. I told myself that if it's meant to be, it will be. I have to keep going and that's just what I did. I told my husband what they said and we were literally on the same page. We didn't obsess over what the results may or may not be. We knew God would bless us with another child when the time was right. In fact, we went out that weekend and had a blast! We celebrated one of his closest friends' birthdays and went out with his brothers and my friend Kelli to celebrate his middle brother's birthday. Then Monday rolled around and my primary care physician scheduled a virtual appointment with me. Our appointment came and she gave me my results. We were 100% pregnant without a shadow of doubt. She said she wanted to tell me over video so she could see my face and make it more personal.

My first time meeting her was after the loss of my son. She shared with me that she lost her son as well, a few days after he made it on earth, due to complications. Though we experienced loss slightly differently, it was still child loss, so we could relate to one another. She had since given birth to another child and she poured so much faith and hope into me with my news. I was ecstatic to know this was really real. After sharing the definitive news with my husband, we literally were in bliss.

Seven weeks later, my husband wanted to take a weekend trip to visit his parents with one of his brothers and I was totally fine with this. It wasn't until he left that anxiety and ptsd hit me like a ton of bricks. I was not okay. It was scary to be alone in the house while pregnant again. I kept thinking something was going to happen to the baby while he was gone, like last time. It was awful. The only way I got to sleep that night was to let a sermon play over and over in the background on my television and to sleep on his side of the bed. He came back the next day and I told him he couldn't go on any more trips while I was pregnant. He didn't.

I am super grateful to have the opportunity to carry one of God's gifts yet again. I definitely don't take this opportunity lightly. I will say pregnancy after a loss is not easy and I'd never sugarcoat that. Though everyone is different, I'd imagine you may experience a little anxiety while pregnant the next go round, and that is normal. One of the things I did differently was having a Doppler at home to ease my anxious thoughts. When the Doppler wasn't enough, if for any reason I had trouble locating the baby's heartbeat, or anytime I felt off for any reason, I went to get checked out right away to ensure my baby was doing well.

One time I went in on Christmas Day for sharp pains in my stomach at 12 weeks. It could've been gas, but I wasn't going to chance it. Come to find out, I had COVID-19. I had them do an ultrasound, and my baby was fine. I had prayer warriors like my Mom, Grandmother, Godmothers, and my Godfather constantly calling to pray with me and reassure me that the baby and I would be just fine, and I trusted that. Now I know everyone may not have several support persons but even if you had one around, I assure you it makes the world of difference to walk through difficult times with someone by your side. My husband was also a rockstar for waiting on me hand and foot. Somehow he never caught COVID-19 and I was so sure I got it from him because he was the one exposed. That's still questionable to me to this day but I will say I kept saying I might have COVID-19 before I found out. He kept saying, "Oh well don't put that on me, I don't have that." He was so certain, even when he was super congested and coughing his brains out all night. I guess it's true. Words are powerful.

Ok I got a little off track with that COVID-19 ordeal. So I said all that to say: do whatever you need to do to ensure the health of you and your baby. It's never too much in my opinion. Also the enemy really started trying me extra hard, especially around the second trimester. I was having so many negative thoughts about my pregnancy and I tried to ignore them until one day I heard the Holy Spirit say, "Speak out loud against every negative thought that comes to your mind. That's just what I did. It takes me back to James 4:7, which says, ". . . Resist the devil and he will flee from you." I had to walk in my authority and not allow him the time of day to infiltrate my mind with thoughts that had no place in my orbit. It made a world of difference. I felt so empowered.

One day, around my 20th week, I started feeling really good. I actually felt like sharing our news this day for whatever reason and so I did. I had no idea that a cutesy little reveal video would go somewhat viral in the maternity world of social media, but it did. I had several mothers reach out to me privately on Instagram for advice or to share their story with me. I felt completely honored that God chose to use me to relate to someone else. I was able to speak on my past experiences and give advice from my perspective on healing gracefully and beautifully. I encourage you if you have experienced what I have or something similar, which I'm sure you have if you're reading this, or maybe not. But I want to assure you that God will use you and anything you've been through to help someone else if you allow Him to. I honestly think that's a beautiful thing.

I advocated for myself a ton during this pregnancy. I had them draw labs for cholestasis (a pregnancy liver disease) since it showed up in my last pregnancy unknowingly. None of my doctors cared to draw labs for this because I didn't show typical symptoms. But I insisted. Come to find out, I indeed had it once again. I didn't get the typical itchiness but I did however have upper right quadrant pain which is a less common symptom that no one ever put together until my diagnosis came back. Also, my High Risk Specialist ran a test for Antiphospholipid Syndrome (APS) something doctors don't typically test you for unless you've experienced a stillborn or several miscarriages. APS is a blood clotting disorder. My results came back inconclusive. I wasn't negative or positive for it. My results were pretty much in the gray area. The doctor advised that this could be normal but to be on the side of caution I should start taking the medication for this which was a daily injection my husband had to administer in an intravenous part of my stomach every single day. About 2 months passed and they ran the test again. The results read inconclusive yet again. This time the advice from my doctor's office was "It's up to you. You can continue taking the injection," which was called Enoxaparin, a burning blood thinner or "you can stop." I decided to stay on the side of caution due to my last outcome of losing our son. I kept taking those injections daily and they burrrrrned so bad that sometimes I cried. My husband injected me with that burning liquid once everyday at around the same time in my belly and because I'm dramatic I made a big deal everyday from 12 weeks of pregnancy until the day before I gave birth. Each day I'd say a quick prayer right before our injection session then I would play a gospel song. After the song was going I would have to find a focal point to focus on so that I could stay as still as possible to ensure I didn't hurt myself or make it more difficult on my husband to administer. He would get so annoyed sometimes at how much prep I had to do to amp myself up for this shot. Every time he seemed annoyed I reiterated to him how unhelpful that was and how he just needs to be ready when I'm ready because I'm the one putting my body through the ringer to bring forth life. Now looking back my tone might not have always been the best but I blame that on the hormones.

Ladies, I can't stress this enough: Always advocate for you and your child, and always educate yourselves! Carrying a child is no easy feat but there is so much that flies under the radar that I urge everyone to stay on top of getting labs drawn and checking anything that doesn't seem normal. All questions are good questions and nothing is ever too silly or ridiculous to check up on. Your maternal health is important. The more knowledge you have and questions you ask, the better outcomes for care you will most likely get. If you don't feel you are getting what you need from a provider or don't feel safe, switch!

This pregnancy has been all about advocating for myself properly, putting anxiety in check, leaning on the Lord, lots of praying with my husband even in the middle of the night, and more consistent monitoring from both my OB and High Risk Specialist. Whenever I felt I needed more monitoring or an extra appointment, I always asked. This may seem excessive to some and it probably was, but I didn't care. I was going to do everything I possibly could to ensure her arrival. Honestly, it was all God. I had to be super dependent and trust that He would see us through this. And He has. I'm currently in the hospital as I write this, going through an induction due to me having cholestasis while pregnant. We are so excited to meet our new bundle of joy who will be born just about three weeks after her brother should she arrive tomorrow! *Yep, we're having a girl! I'll tell you her name once she's born!*

♦♦♦

When our son's birthday rolled around on May 27th, I knew I still wanted to celebrate him. Something intimate with just my husband and I. We originally planned to say a prayer and do a balloon release to the sky but guess what – Party City didn't have any helium that evening. What in the world? So I decided to buy him a nice vanilla cupcake with white icing and white sprinkles. We got home, added a candle, lit it, and sang him Happy Birthday. I didn't expect to get so emotional, but I did, right in the midst of singing. I realized I'm literally singing Happy Birthday to someone who is not here in the physical, my angel, and not my living child. That was a harsh reality, a difficult pill to swallow. To think to myself, "Wow he would've been an entire one year old today." I let my emotions roll in fiercely, looked through his keepsake with all his things, and talked to him out loud as I'm sure his spirit was around.

After celebrating his first heavenly birthday, I realized how far God had allowed me to come. I was now blessed to carry my second child, his sister. She is still living in my womb and when she's born she gets to have a personal angel watching over her. Her big brother, DJ.

Now after the outcome I had with my son I didn't want to do a lot of things the same nor did I seek answers from anyone except God. I didn't really seek a prophetic word this time around, I didn't write anything in my journal, I just held on to the belief that God wouldn't allow me to endure this pain again and accepted encouragement. Well one day my car had a bad oil leak so we rushed it over to a nearby Jiffy Lube. While I was waiting on my car to be tended to I saw a young lady with a jeep almost identical to mine. Oh yeah I got a new car at the top of the year. Since I described my car I had while I was pregnant with my son at the beginning of this book. Ok, anyways so I sit down on this bench outside and I feel in my spirit that this young lady has something she wants to say to me but I didn't know what. Eventually she breaks the ice by asking me "Are you having a boy or girl?" I told her "girl" and she smiled. She said "Is this your first?" I said "no, this is my second. My son is in heaven . He was stillborn" She said "ok, did his name start with a D" In my head I was like "ok, here we go." I was on guard. I was talking to God like please help me discern what's right or not and to block my energy from receiving anything off putting. You have to be careful. People are crazy out here and there are all kinds of spirits roaming around this earth. You better be mindful of which ones you allow around you even if they say they follow Christ. I'm not trying to scare you, I just want you to be aware. Sometimes wicked spirits can be disguised as nice people. Trust me, I've had an encounter with a wicked spirit in church of all places. This woman literally yelled out a statement to me in a bathroom line. Please folks don't put so much stock in thinking people in church are going to be perfect. They won't. They will disappoint you because they are human. I hear about church hurt all the time and I can see how many people end up leaving God's house because of it. I hate that it happens but if you already know no one is perfect, including churchgoers, and that wickedness can be anywhere and in anyone. You'll never get disappointed again. You just need to ask God for the gift of discernment. It's actually important to be able to discern spirits and intentions within those around you. Discernment is everything and hasn't failed me yet. Ok, let me stop. I went wayyyy to the left and I can feel myself about to get very churchy in a minute. I'll turn this whole book into a sermon. Nah I'm kidding, pastoring is not my calling. Listen, you better be super certain God called you to lead a church because did you know in the Bible it says he will judge them twice as hard (woo chile).

Ok, back to the story – so after she asked me about the first letter of my son's name I answered her back with "yes, his name is DJ and it stands for Devon Jr." She then smiled and said, "It's great that you acknowledge him. He's so happy for his sister to get here. Everything you went through, all those nights of praying and that time you sat there and contemplated turning your back on God, but you didn't. God was testing your faith. Your next season is going to be good." She then went on to say, "I'm sorry if this is weird." I was like, "No, not at all. I'm glad you told me all of that. It was reassuring." It was like God gave me a gentle hug through her words. Like yes I see you and what you went through was not in vain. She was very gentle with her approach and her language. I can tell she was new to exercising her gift of prophecy. She told me about the friends she's lost because of her sharing things with them she saw, and when it happened, they felt weirded out by her or mad at her. Now as I was talking to her my discerning spirit allowed me to soften up and receive. I could have hardened my heart because my last prophecy seemed to not go as stated, but to be honest, I still don't have the answers on that. Those same things could manifest in a future son or maybe not, but God will show me the answer to that when and if he gets ready.

Afterword

I hope if you have experienced child loss like me or something similar that you still hold on to hope. That you still choose to believe again, and that you realize you are undoubtedly worthy of having a rainbow baby, rainbow twins, triplets, quadruplets, or a child in a totally different way other than birthing them IF that is your heart's desire.

Always honor your angel baby **your** way. If your angel baby was your first, you are still a mother. Your journey to motherhood just looks a lot different from others, and that's ok. It's ok to still be emotional months and even years later. Each tear you shed is just an expression of the love you have for your child rolling in from the depths of your soul presenting to the surface.

After it was all said and done and I was living with the truth of the loss of my son, I didn't lose joy. Joy restored itself within me. And eventually hope did as well. I believe that by having a relationship with God and allowing Him to truly step in, take the wheel, take over and order my steps, is what got me through and will get you through should you be facing the same or a similar situation that I had.

I remember I had a dream when I was pregnant about a t-shirt and on it, it said, “Order My Steps.” And I remember I listened to that song over and over again and I thought, “This is just a shirt I’m supposed to make” because I had an Etsy shop at the time so I made the shirt. It was so vivid in my dream. Little did I know that I would have to hang on to those words, and wearing those words, looking at those words often, and that verse that I couldn't shake, Jeremiah 29:11. All these things that I thought meant or were for something else really led up to the moment of me losing my son and having to hold on to God truly ordering my steps, and me remembering that I asked him to use me. I asked Him to use me as a vessel to help others. I asked Him for this. I didn’t ask Him to take my son, no I did not. But I did ask Him to use me in a mighty way and I did ask Him to order my steps. So we can say, “Be careful what you ask for.” But isn’t that what we’re here for anyway?

Aren't we here to help our brothers and sisters? Aren't we here to help someone else out of a dark space when we've made it back to the light? Isn't that what it's all about? Isn't that why God placed us here? For a purpose? On purpose. To do something in the world, to make a change in the world. To serve God.

So remember that as you're going through what you're going through. And though it's hard, and though it does not change how you feel, remember that God truly does have a purpose in everything that He does in our lives.

Yes, He gives us freedom of choice to choose and make choices. But when your world is shaken and truly out of your control and you can't even make a choice about it, allow God to move. Allow Him to order your steps. You have to surrender at that point.

I overcame by remembering that my life is not my own, and that I belong to God. That He put me here for a reason and that He does things intentionally. That He's going to use this. That's what got me through, knowing God did this on purpose. And I know that's probably not the most popular thing to say and I know some people won't agree. But for me, I had to stand on that. And I had to stand on faith in knowing, "Well, God still promised me a child to raise. And I believe He'll bless me with a child to raise."

So, even though it ended the way that it did, I believed God would still give us a rainbow baby. And He did. Her name is Wynter and she's absolutely beautiful. This is our kid we dreamed and talked about when we were in college. We named her in college. And here we are almost 9-10 years later and she's here.

But we also dreamed of having a son. And we do have a son. I told God I only wanted two kids. Well, He's funny. Who knows, maybe we'll have more. You know they say, "If you want to make God laugh, tell Him your plans."

I want to encourage you to allow those around you to be there for you. Don't shut them out. Let people help you. But have discernment about it. I had people that seemed like they truly cared, invited me to lunch with gifts, but in reality it was totally different. They wanted something out of me. It almost felt like they were using my pain as an opportunity. But nonetheless, have discernment. Because the people that God brought into my life, some of them I've known for my entire life and some of them were people I hadn't known long at all.. And they stepped in for me and Devon like a nice vegan ice cream cone on a hot, sunny day (I don't eat dairy so vegan ice cream will always sound better to me!). Just so satisfying and them knowing exactly what we needed when we needed it. I had to take a step back and realize there was even a blessing in God removing people out of my life and putting new people in that place.

Try not to let your heart harden. Keep it soft and malleable. Remember to view your emotions as if they are like water. Let them flow in and flow out, like a tide or a wave. Feel everything.

You're like the sand. You are still. The water's washing up over you, then the water leaves and the sand dries back up from the sun, then the ocean water comes rushing back. That's how your emotions may feel every day. Then eventually the water gets to a point where it just kind of wades. That's when you've gotten to a new level in your healing journey and you're kind of wading. What happened has happened, you're living with it. And you're wading. Wading with your emotions. Just kind of swaying. Not leaving, not in an up and down motion, but you're there. You're just there.

Now the sun is beaming on the water and you're still on the sand. Your emotions are there on top of you. Now the sun has come in to warm up the surface. So now maybe you can warm up to getting back to your life. So just know there's always light that will come out, even at nighttime when the water's wading in and the tides are high and emotions are high. Remember that morning will break. The sun is going to come out. Your emotions will settle. You have to allow healing. You have to allow yourself to heal beautifully. Because you can indeed heal ugly, but if you heal beautifully, there's so much life to live. Tragedy is going to happen and you'll realize things are going to happen to everyone at different times in their lives and it's all about how you carry it. You have a choice in the way you decide to carry it. If you allow God to really move in your life, He will show you how to carry it. And He'll place people there to help you along.

Now that my daughter is here, our rainbow baby, she has restored hope in a new way. Though I had it before, now I see it physically in the flesh. It's amazing. It's absolutely amazing. And I believe that God allowed us to have her at this time for a reason. She's so special to so many people, not even just us. It's an honor to parent a child. And even if God has made it to where you can no longer carry, remember that there's always another way for you to get that child you deserve and will love. And there's a reason God set it up that way for you, and for that child.

I learned a lot from having a little extra time without a child to raise. I learned that I may not have made me a priority the first go round. I was convinced I really was going to have to give up my dreams at least for a long time. My mindset surrounding motherhood was delusional. I was borrowing from what I saw others do. This time around, I demanded it. I demanded my time. I mean if you have any type of help you may as well use it. God blessed me with a capable husband and we asked my Mom to stay with us for extended periods so that I could still work on my dreams and goals. Childcare is astronomical in my area. My Mom freed us up on nights if I had an acting class or my husband had to go coach simultaneously and on weekends where we might want to go on a date. We all work full time during the week. I work from home and care for baby girl and the times my Mom was staying with us, if I had a really important meeting we would try to juggle who looked after her if she wasn't down for a nap. Teamwork makes the dream work. Though it's very hard to carve out the time you need to take a breather or work on your personal goals with a new baby, it is possible. Life just continues on with our new little ones added along for the ride. Everyone's circumstances are different but I truly do believe where there is a will there's a way. I'm very conscious of the time I need for myself. I'm very conscious that I need to take care of myself. I'm very conscious of the things I still want to do because I want my daughter to see the possibility of what is achievable through me. I just want to be a living example for her.

Children imitate everything. So not just for her but for myself, I still have hopes and dreams for my life. That has not changed. My daughter is now along for the journey, to witness it. But I still have to do all the other things God has called me to do. I cannot forget myself in motherhood. I have to embrace motherhood and know that it has definitely changed my life. But everything else still gets to be added in. And it's so beautiful the way that God will allow your world to change like that, to bring a new life in and grant you with the responsibility of raising up another vessel for him and with him. Now that's a task! A task you were handpicked and specifically assigned to in order to help complete God's plan. He chose us and that's a true honor!

Postpartum Guide for Mamas Who Have Experienced Loss

If you're a mama taking care of yourself after experiencing loss, this guide is for you. Postpartum is challenging for every mom, but it's different when you're also processing grief. I hope this guide helps you to navigate your postpartum journey, no matter what that looks like for you.

Day 1:

After I had DJ, I put on two bras as soon as I left the hospital. I started using cabbage the next day, only on my nipples, to relieve pain and breast swelling. I then moved on to the whole leaf to cover my entire breast area. When doing this, remember to crunch the leaves to break down the veins.

Day 3:

On Day 3, I started using ice packs because I had gone from a D cup to almost busting out of a DD. I probably could've gone for an E. To stop my milk from coming in, I binded with an Ace bandage and finally moved on to a tight zip-up sports bra from Target.

I also came across the "No More Milk Tea" by Earth Mama Organic, which I drank three times a day from days 2-8. My midwife told me it may take up to 10 days to get any relief and for my boobs to feel normal again.

Days 5-6:

By this time, I was at my peak of fullness. I saw the golden milk spill out just a little while also being in excruciating pain from engorgement. Day 6 I had the worst throbbing and sharp pain in my smallest and leakiest boob. Again, ice and cold cabbage were very soothing during this time.

I have a legal registered medical card so I utilized medical cannabis as pain relief since the prescribed pain meds weren't effective for me. It became super painful to dry up my milk. Remember I'm just sharing what has helped me from my own experience in hopes that some if not all of these tips can be helpful to you or someone you know. My midwife told me to avoid my breasts completely when showering. I was not to stimulate them at all because we didn't want to give my body any idea to make more milk than it already was. I was instructed not to pump because more would produce, and not to squeeze (which was fine by me because they were so sensitive and hard as rocks I was literally afraid they might explode at some point). It makes me squeamish just saying that as my memory rushes back. But hey, I'm here to be candid and honest with you. I want you to know what may be coming your way so you're prepared, unless you're already at this stage.

Also, be aware of any flu-like symptoms, like fatigue, lumps, pus draining from the nipple or extreme unbearable pain. Go get checked to make sure you don't have mastitis. This is a breast infection that can happen, so watch out for it.

What you will need:

To Dry up Milk:

Earth Mama Organic – "No More Milk Tea"

Cabbage Leaves

Zip-up sports bras (or any zip-up bra that is 1-2 sizes bigger than your size after delivery)

An Ace bandage to bind your breasts

For Your Vagina:

Witch Hazel Pads

Peri Peri Bottle

Giant Panties, Adult diapers, and disposable hospital-like undies

Long pads for heavy bleeding

Instant Ice Maxi Pads

Perineal healing spray

For Your Stomach:

Waist Binder (I recommend the Bengkung belly binder, which I purchased on Etsy and via Sacred Birth Doula on Amazon)

For your mental health:

You may need to recite affirmations. I recommend an affirming positive playlist of songs to play every morning when you wake up.

I also strongly recommend therapy.

If you're experiencing loss I suggest journaling or recording your thoughts and feelings. You have to get it out of your head or even have a go-to person you can vent to at any time.

A support system is **vital**. The number of people supporting you isn't what's important. It's about the quality, spirit, and intention of the person. Use wisdom with who you choose to share with outside of your therapist.

Lastly, I recommend spending time with God, even if you're in a rocky place because you don't understand why your loss took place. You may not understand now or to be honest you may not ever. I'm not God and we all have a different journey, but I do believe God allows everything to happen for a purpose.

Acknowledgements

I would like to start off by thanking my super supportive husband, Devon Wright-Nelson, for encouraging me to finish writing this book even while I was pregnant with our daughter. You kept telling me that my story will help so many others. You were so excited about the book that you planned out my book signing before I was even done with the first chapter. I'm so blessed to have you. Thank you for always holding me accountable and cheering me on. I love you so much.

I would also like to thank my mother, Shandrica Sheppard, for always listening to me. You've always given me a safe space to share my feelings and entire truth without judgment, ever since I was a child. Thank you for always making me feel heard and understood. You are the reason I can be so transparent and share my life testimonies. Thank you for always leading me to God and being a great example of a loving Mother.

I have to thank my Editor, Kanisha Parker at Genesis Mass Media Group. Kanisha thank you thank you for believing in my book from the very beginning. You have been extra patient with me in seeing this to completion. I loved that we always kept God in the center of every conversation and strategy. You even helped me name the book! Thank you!

About the Author

Summyr Wright- Nelson is a dynamic writer, lifestyle influencer, and actress. She's from Augusta, Georgia and lived in the Washington, DC area during the events of this book and at the time of writing this book with her husband, Devon; her son in heaven, DJ; and her daughter Wynter Rayne Wright-Nelson. She's no stranger to sharing her experiences with others as she always believes that our testimonies can be a beautiful inspiration and sense of hope for someone else.

Made in the USA
Columbia, SC
30 March 2025

55825845R00071